ONE FRAME
AT A TIME

100+ TIPS TO IMPROVE
YOUR BOWLING GAME

Tyrel Rose
and
Bill Sempsrott

BTM Digital Media, LLC

ISBN: 9798864549384

Published by BTM Digital Media, LLC
www.bowlingthismonth.com

*To our wives, children, and parents, for inspiring us and
supporting us in all of life's adventures.*

CONTENTS

INTRODUCTION

Hello, reader! Thank you for buying this book.

Over the years, *Bowling This Month* has published thousands of in-depth instructional and technical articles to help bowlers improve their games. Starting as a print magazine in 1994 and now a digital publication, *Bowling This Month* is a world-renowned resource for bowlers looking to improve.

This book is the culmination of our effort to take some of *Bowling This Month*'s best advice and present it in easy-to-read tips, so you can apply them in your next practice or league session.

We've compiled some of our best and most popular tips from recent years and created new, exclusive tips for this book that you can't find anywhere else.

The goal here isn't for you to read this book cover-to-cover. It's more of a manual, so you can focus on the tip that applies to you right away.

Like with any good coaching, the idea is to work on one thing at a time and move on to the next tip when you're ready. Sometimes, that will mean working through several tips in a week. Other times, it will mean working on one skill for several weeks.

If you're struggling with your pre-shot routine, flip to the mental game section and find a tip to improve your routine, or an element of it, such as visualization.

If you're struggling with your release, your lane play, or your spare shooting, there are tips for you as well.

If you're a beginning bowler just wanting to know some of the basics of bowling balls, we've got you covered.

Whatever the case, and wherever you are on your bowling journey, there are tips in here to help you improve and to remind you of things you may have forgotten.

This isn't your typical book.

Go ahead: highlight key points, take notes, and dog-ear the pages. Carry it around in your bag to review key pages before league night or a tournament.

This book is here for you to use, to abuse, and to help you improve your game.

    –Tyrel and Bill

SECTION 1

THE PHYSICAL
GAME

The bowling approach has evolved quite a bit since the classic days of Dick Weber. In fact, many people refer to the two styles as the "classic style" and the "modern style" of bowling.

The modern game is significantly more dynamic, and that applies to both the one-handed style and the powerful two-handed style that has become popular in recent years. The tips in this book focus mostly on the one-handed game, but there are some tips that apply to both groups.

One of the key things to remember and keep in mind about the modern game is the importance of generating higher ball speeds and more revs than bowlers from decades ago.

With equipment that is much more aggressive than in previous generations, there is a need for more speed in order to counteract the amount of hook that modern bowling balls can generate. With this evolution, bowlers and coaches have a better grasp of biomechanics to help minimize strain on the body.

To give a brief comparison, here are some of the key differences between the classic style and the modern game.

Footwork
It wasn't that long ago that most bowlers used four steps. Nowadays, to get more momentum, bowlers will generally use five steps, or even more. This has changed how we describe timing because the ball motion that used to start on the first step now starts on the second step.

Armswing
The modern armswing features a higher backswing that is generally much higher than the classic game. Typically, the modern one-handed backswing is now

head-height or even a bit higher compared to the shoulder-height armswings of yesteryear.

This puts a lot more strain on the shoulder joint and requires good body position to help alleviate some of the stress.

Body Position

The modern body position is much more dynamic. We see more forward lean and core rotation during the approach. The release position features more spine tilt and a lowered bowling shoulder for better leverage.

In all, the modern game features many of the same requirements, such as balance and timing, but the positions and movements have evolved thanks to modern equipment and a better understanding of the human body.

Improving Your Balance

Bowling is a dynamic sport. With so many moving parts, achieving proper balance at the foul line can be difficult. Here are a few things you can do to improve your stability at the line:

- **Strengthen your legs and core**: Improving your poor balance isn't always related to bowling skill. It might instead be about establishing a strong base through appropriate exercises to strengthen and mobilize your legs and core.
- **Work on your timing**: In many cases, bad balance at the line is the result of timing issues that cause poor mechanics.
- **Find your CG**: Your center of gravity is near your belly button. This must be centered over your slide foot. It can look different for different bowlers, so find your ideal finish position and work to make it consistent.

Tips for Increasing Your Ball Speed

Many bowlers, including rev-dominant players, can frequently find themselves in a position where they need a bit more speed. Here are a few tips to help you achieve just that:

- **Use momentum**: Shift your weight just as you start your approach, leaning forward and putting the weight on your toes to help increase your foot speed.
- **Move back on the approach**: A longer approach can yield longer strides to help generate more speed.
- **Increase the height of your backswing**: Generate more swing speed by creating a higher backswing. Get more momentum in the ball start to help the ball rise higher at its peak.

Reducing ball speed for those who are speed-dominant would require the opposite: shifting your weight back onto your heels in the stance; starting closer to the foul line; and lowering the height of your backswing.

Using Physical Triggers Effectively

While many bowlers look for the stance to be completely stationary, a trigger is a movement that can be used to help create a smooth transition from standing still to moving forward. For example, Pete Weber would tap his finger on the ball before he started walking.

Here are a few tips for using a trigger effectively to improve your consistency:

- Triggers are not movement for the sake of movement. They often start out unconsciously, but they become a purposeful piece of your routine.
- Bowlers should have no more than one trigger. Too much movement will cause misalignment and inconsistency.
- The trigger can support an important physical cue, such as moving/tucking the elbow or relaxing the shoulder to support a swing thought about a relaxed armswing.

Increasing Your Rev Rate

The release is the culmination of the entire approach, where bowlers impart speed and revolutions to the bowling ball. With this in mind, here are a few tips to help you increase your rev rate:

- **Optimize your timing and swing plane**: A straight swing and good timing will lead to a better overall body position to maximize your release efficiency.
- **Check your grip**: The modern release typically has more forward pitch in the thumb and more reverse pitch in the fingers to keep the hand relaxed for more quickness through the release.
- **Practice the wrist motion**: Even without a bowling ball, you can practice the modern load/unload release with everyday objects or specific release training tools to master the timing of cupping and uncupping the wrist.

Improving Your Accuracy

When it comes to the sport of bowling, everyone wants to improve their accuracy, which is the ability to hit a specific target repeatedly.

In bowling, this is an essential part of the recipe for improving your average, making cuts, and winning tournaments. Here are three things you can do to improve your accuracy:

- **Proper alignment**: Make sure your hips, shoulders, knees, and feet are properly aligned with your desired ball path.
- **Straight swing**: With few exceptions, a consistently straight swing is a key element of good accuracy.
- **Consistent timing**: Work on having a repeatable approach that gets you and the ball to the line the same way every time. This helps minimize timing variations that will affect your launch angle.

Tips for a Free Armswing

Achieving a free armswing is synonymous with removing tension from your hand and arm. When working on achieving a free armswing, reducing tension starts even before we perform the ball start.

To get a swing with zero wasted energy and minimal tension, try these tips:

- Get your grip checked. A well-fitted ball reduces grip pressure, which reduces tension in the swing.
- In the stance, support the weight of the bowling ball with your non-bowling hand. There's no perfect ratio, so find a balance that works for you.
- Start the ball and allow gravity to drop the ball into the backswing. Tension at the start of the swing will stay there throughout.

Finger Position Release Adjustments

Changing your ball roll isn't always about making a complete hand position change. There is also value in fine-tuning your release through small index finger and pinky finger placement adjustments:

- The wider you spread your index finger, the more likely you will come around the ball more. The tighter it is to your middle finger, the more forward roll you will tend to have.
- The pinky works in the opposite way. Spreading your pinky finger promotes forward roll, while keeping it tight promotes higher axis rotation.
- Maximum potential side roll comes from a spread index finger and a tucked pinky finger.

Use different finger position combinations to fine-tune your ball reaction as needed.

Ball Position in the Stance

A bowler's stance is often as unique as they are. You'd be hard-pressed to find two identical start positions, even among bowlers developed by the same coach. That said, one of the constants of a good start position is an optimal ball position in the stance:

- Keep the elbow bend at less than 90 degrees and place weight into the supporting hand to help reduce muscle tension.
- The ball should be placed directly under the ball-side shoulder, with the shoulders square to the target line.
- Minimize grip pressure by relaxing the bowling hand before starting the approach.

In short, bowlers should avoid a ball position that creates too much tension or sets the ball on the wrong path before the bowler starts walking.

Because of the differences in body shape, arm length, etc., this will look different for each bowler, but the ball should be in a good position relative to their desired target line.

Small Tricks to Increase Your Speed

Whether you want to permanently increase your ball speed or you simply want the option of using a higher speed to adapt to drier conditions, many bowlers have found themselves with a need for speed.

While most coaches will correctly point to a higher backswing and/or faster feet to create more ball speed, there are a few other details that can help a bowler on their journey to achieving this goal.

- **Check your grip**: Reducing your grip pressure will loosen up your swing and allow for more potential speed.
- **Lean forward**: Shifting your center of gravity forward will get your feet going faster, which is a key element of generating more ball speed.
- **Slide more**: Creating a longer slide can allow for better transfer of energy to the ball, resulting in more speed.

Freeing Up Your Armswing

A bowler's footwork often follows the swing: a slow swing results in slower feet, while a loose swing results in faster feet.

The first step to generating more momentum (and using less muscle tension) is to free up your swing and let your legs play catch-up:

- Do swing drills with something in your hand other than a bowling ball. Another heavy object will force you out of your "bowling brain" and allow you to perform the movement more naturally.
- Incorporate this object into a mock approach, intentionally trying to go to the line more quickly. Next, try it with your bowling ball.
- As your swing speeds up, you'll likely feel uncomfortable. Just keep going. Use your feet to chase after the ball.

Understanding Loft

Manipulating your loft can be challenging. Whether you're trying to permanently adjust the amount of your loft or develop the skill to change it on demand for different conditions, the same basic principles apply.

Loft is how far onto the lane the ball is projected before it lands. It is affected both by the height of the release point and by when the ball is released in the swing:

- Adjusting the height of the release is a matter of changing the release position by modifying how much knee and hip bend you use. Standing taller will result in more loft.
- The point at which the ball is released in the swing will depend on the quality of the fit, so check that first.
- Work to release the ball in the flat spot of the swing to reduce loft, and practice releasing slightly on the upswing to increase it.

Keys to the Release

A consistent release is one of the most important elements of the sport of bowling. The release is your last point of contact with the bowling ball, where you transfer energy in the form of ball speed and revolutions.

Improvements to your release can come from many different parts of your game. A straight swing and good body position are paramount to a powerful and consistent release.

When working to improve your rev rate or your release consistency, remember the following:

- Consistency comes from effective technique. Focus on a loose swing and sound fundamentals.
- Check your grip fit. A relaxed hand can move faster and impart more revolutions.
- Consistency is more important than power. It's better to have the same consistent rev rate, even if it's a bit lower, than to be inconsistent while trying to max out every time.

Improving Timing Consistency

Good timing is essential to good bowling. But what is good timing?

Put simply, good timing is consistent timing that allows you to repeat shots. To be a more consistent shotmaker, you need consistent timing at the release point. To achieve this, there are two points in the swing you should be checking: the ball start and the swing apex.

The ball start should be consistently timed based on the height of the swing. Bowlers with higher backswings will generally need to get the ball started sooner than those with lower backswings.

The ball should reach the top of the swing, pause briefly, and then come back down. The best way to achieve this is to allow gravity to start it on the way down. Do swing drills to practice achieving a "weightless" feeling at the top of the backswing and as the ball starts its downward path.

Improving Your Finish Position

The finish position is generally influenced by the footwork, timing, and swing that come before it. However, a bowler can still improve their finish position by isolating a few elements of the movement, which can then influence positions earlier in the approach.

Some of the elements of the finish position that can be improved with drills include the following:

- **The follow through**: Reach long and low, instead of up.
- **Center of gravity**: Your center of gravity should be directly above your slide foot, with the weight evenly placed over the mid-foot.
- **Posture**: Focus on keeping your posture upright enough so that your head is above your slide foot throughout the release.

Release drills at the foul line or one-step slide drills are best for this kind of work.

Stance and Ball Speed

The bowler's stance affects the entire approach. Alignment, ball position, and foot placement all impact aspects of the delivery of the ball. One simple element of the start position can also have a big impact on your ball speed.

If you are looking to reduce your ball speed, it helps to lean back in the approach, centering your weight more on your heels. This can slow down your overall rhythm and reduce your ball speed to create more hook without making any other changes.

Starting with the weight more on your toes or leaning forward slightly as you get started will create more forward momentum and increase your ball speed. This is especially useful to bowlers with smaller builds who are trying to get more speed on the ball.

The Crossover Step Drill

The crossover step is the first step with your ball-side foot. It should be relatively short and placed directly in front of your non-ball-side foot. It is the first step in a four-step approach or the second step in a five-step approach. For the purpose of this tip, we'll discuss this drill using a four-step approach.

Taking only one step, perform a "ball start" without the ball to establish the direction and distance. Then step back into your start position. After a few repetitions, add the ball and repeat the process.

For a handy visual reference, place painter's tape on either side of your non-ball-side foot to create a guide for your foot placement. Be sure to ask permission to place tape on the approach and ensure that no residue is left behind to endanger other bowlers.

Keys to an Effective Start Position

The physical game itself originates with the stance, and it can either set you up for success or create problems. Keep these tips in mind to make your stance an effective part of your physical game:

- Ensure that your feet, hips, and shoulders are aligned with your intended ball path.
- Your degree of forward lean will influence your ball speed. Lean back if you want to slow down; lean forward to throw the ball faster.
- Ensure that your ball is in a position for a straight ball path, which will look different depending on your body type. As a rule of thumb, you want the ball in line with or just outside of your hip, but not outside of your shoulder.

Evaluate your stance periodically, either with video or with the help of your coach, and adjust it as needed to make sure your approach is working for you, and not against you.

How to Fix Early Timing

What used to be called "early timing" is now commonly known as "roller timing." Roller timing is the result of the swing getting to the foul line before the slide is completed. While there are several examples of bowlers on the PBA Tour who have/had this timing—such as Marshall Holman, Chris Barnes, and Robert Smith—excessively early timing will often result in loss of balance and a loss of rev rate.

In order to delay timing at the release, most bowlers need to delay their timing earlier in the swing. This can be achieved by one of two things: lengthening the time to complete the swing, or using faster footwork to shorten the approach.

To lengthen the swing, consider working on a later ball start, or using more extension. Both of these can be worked on through the use of the ball start drill. For faster feet, consider leaning more forward in the stance to help you create more forward momentum during the approach.

The cause of early timing can also be mental. With a coach, examine if overthinking might be causing you to slow down and control your movements.

Understanding the Swing Plane

The bowling swing plane can be examined from behind to address any lateral movement as well as from the side to examine how steep it is.

From behind, the ideal swing plane should be straight and in line with the intended target path, with the ball positioned under/behind the head throughout. While some variation is acceptable, once the ball is completely inside or outside the head, you will need to bring it back in line.

More often than not, this is the result of a ball start that is out of line, or muscles in the back being used to lift the ball into the swing. Once the source is identified, you can fix the swing's direction.

From the side, the goal is for the swing to be as smooth into the foul line as possible. Higher swings tend to have steeper downswings, so they should be started farther from the foul line so they can have a shallower descent into the release. Longer slides help to keep the vertical swing plane more shallow, like the bottom of a U, rather than angular like the point of a V.

The Slide Drill

The slide drill, also called a one-step drill, is when the bowler only takes a single step in the approach. This is used to work on release timing, body position, and/or balance at the line.

Start three or four feet from the foul line in your normal starting position. Because you won't be walking, you might need your ball-side foot to be positioned slightly more behind your slide foot.

Swing the ball. The goal isn't to achieve your normal backswing height; instead, lower is better. Once the ball reaches the apex of the swing, you step/slide with your slide foot so the ball is coming down as the foot is moving forward.

This drill can be done one-handed or two-handed. It should be modified as needed in terms of body position to achieve the desired swing direction while focusing on the release phase of the approach.

Keys to Adjusting Axis Rotation

Experienced bowlers will have a natural release that generates their typical amount of axis rotation and rev rate. Changing your axis rotation can be a key component in lane play adjustments. Here are a few options on how to do it:

- Adjust your hand position in the stance. Starting with more of the weight in your bowling hand promotes forward roll. Starting with your hand on the side promotes more side roll.
- Play with your finger positions. Changing how your fingers are placed on the ball affects the roll you will impart. Spreading the index finger, for example, tends to increase axis rotation.
- Some bowlers simply rotate their hand more or less at release without changing anything in their stance.

Like any skill, it takes a lot of practice to manipulate your release. The goal should be to establish at least a few different ball rolls to adapt to changing lane conditions.

Keys to an Effective Body Position

In the second-to-last step of the approach, a bowler's body should be rotated with the arms extended into a T or tilted T position, depending on the height of the backswing. Here are some keys to achieving that position.

- The non-bowling arm should be in front of the body as a mirror of the bowling arm, but with the hand rotated so the thumb is pointed toward the lane.
- The lead shoulder should be approximately under the chin.
- The bowling shoulder should be straight behind the torso, with the ball in line with the head.

For two-handers, this position is very similar, but usually with more forward lean, and the non-bowling arm under the body and across the chest to support the bowling ball in the backswing.

Optimal Release Position

With so many moving parts, achieving an optimal release position can be very difficult. We also don't want to confuse it with the "finish position," which happens after the ball has left the hand.

In the release position, the bowler wants to be in a position of leverage, with the hand, arm, and body in a dynamic position to impart speed and revolutions to the bowling ball.

- At release, the shoulders rotate closed so they are square with the intended path.
- The upper body and trail leg will be on approximately the same angle, leaning toward the intended line.
- The slide leg and the bowling arm will create a V shape.
- The bowling hand should be behind or on the inside half of the ball.

These things are true for both one-handed and two-handed bowlers, with minor variations.

Refining Your Footwork

A bowler's footwork is the foundation of generating ball speed and balance. Proper footwork helps you achieve better rhythm and momentum going into the release. Here are some tips to improve your footwork:

- Beware a large first step: Starting with an overly large step often results in poor timing and deceleration at the end of the approach. Ideally, the first step should be fairly small.
- Use a crossover step: The first step you take with your ball-side foot should be directly in front of the other foot, not beside it.
- Your slide should be directly under your body, usually in the direction of your ball path and angled slightly inwards.

Beyond these key components, the most important aspect of footwork is a sense of rhythm and fluidity. A bowler should be relatively light on their feet, without any one step looking more forceful than another.

Achieving Optimal Timing

The modern one-handed game has very different timing mechanics from bowling of previous eras. Instead of the "out-down-up-through" timing of the classic four-step approach, the modern approach is faster paced, features a higher backswing, and uses more momentum going into the release.

For this reason, optimal timing in the modern game is generally much earlier at the start of the approach compared to the classic game. Here are some of the key timing points for bowlers today:

- The ball start should happen as the toes touch and the heel comes off the ground in the first step of a five-step approach.
- Optimal timing of the start of the backswing occurs when both knees are in line and the arm is vertical, with the ball going backwards past the knee.
- The peak of the swing should happen in the fourth step, with a slight pause before coming down into the release. If there is no pause, the ball is getting there too late.

Fixing Slow Feet

Many bowlers are too slow in their approach. This is a normal reaction to constantly being warned against being too fast, but an overly methodical approach can be just as detrimental.

One of the main causes of this for beginners is overthinking. This happens because the bowling approach is one of the most complex movements in sports. You need to synchronize your ball start with your footwork, keep your swing straight, and try to roll the ball over your target. There's a lot to think about.

For intermediate and advanced bowlers, the cause is much the same, but it's a different kind of thought process. Often the overthinking stems from analysis of the lane play or self-doubt in the execution.

The solution is much the same for both groups. The goal should be to simply think about one cue, such as the ball start, or the target, and let things flow from there.

Reducing how much you are trying to control in the approach will result in a more fluid movement and more accuracy in the long run.

SECTION 2

EQUIPMENT, LAYOUTS, AND FITTING

Bowling equipment has evolved quite a bit since its inception. In this section, we discuss some of the key aspects of bowling ball technology, fitting, and layouts for the modern game.

Historically, bowling balls had cores inside that were only meant to offset the weight that would be removed from drilling holes. But as these cores have become more complex, so have drilling techniques.

Not that long ago, most layouts were based mostly on the hand placement, with the core being positioned relative to the palm. Modern techniques require that drillers know and use the bowler's positive axis point.

The positive axis point, or PAP, is a point on the ball that represents its axis of rotation as it is being released. It is based on the oil line or track of the bowling ball. PAPs differs for bowlers based on how they release the ball, and the PAP is the starting point for modern layouts.

In addition to drilling techniques that have changed, the correct methods for fitting and gripping the bowling ball have also evolved. The "old-school" release was one where the bowler lifted their fingers and closed their hand as they released the ball. As such, spans were generally fairly long, stretching out the fingers, with hole angles (pitches) that allowed the thumb to exit quickly.

The modern release is much more dynamic, with more emphasis placed on the extension of the fingers during the release. Old techniques with a stretched-out hand would cause serious injury over time, so modern fitting has adapted. Spans are generally shorter, with more forward pitch in the thumb and more reverse in the fingers, for a more relaxed grip.

Most importantly for lane play, bowling ball coverstocks have evolved quite a bit. Since the introduction of reactive resin bowling balls in the early 1990s, classic urethane balls became obsolete.

However, as reactive bowling balls have become more and more aggressive, a new modern wave of urethane bowling balls have come back to popularity. With modern cores and manufacturing techniques, these urethane balls hook more than their predecessors from the 1980s.

Altogether, bowling equipment is much more complex than it used to be, so pro shop operators and their expertise are a vital part of improving and understanding the game.

Choosing a Pro Shop

There are plenty of options when it comes to getting your equipment drilled. For new and experienced bowlers alike, the choice can be difficult. Aside from having a certification, here are a few things to look for when considering who to trust with your equipment:

- A pro shop professional should ask to watch you bowl to get an idea of your game when suggesting equipment or changes to your grip.
- Is the work area tidy? There will always be a certain amount of dust in a pro shop, but a professional who takes good care of their workspace is likely to take good care of you.
- If a ball driller's bowling hand is in good shape, it's a good sign that their fitting and drilling skills will keep your hand feeling good as well.

Managing Your Accessories

Almost every bowler uses some sort of accessories to go along with their all-important arsenal of bowling balls. Do you replace your accessories often? How prepared are you when you go to a tournament?

Finger inserts, interchangeable shoe soles and heels, and abrasive pads all wear out eventually and need to be replaced at regular intervals. Keep track of the number of times you've used your abrasive pads so they can be replaced before they lose effectiveness. Keep an eye on your soles and heels and replace them as needed.

Even if you're not someone whose skin rips often, you should always have some kind of protective tape or liquid skin patch in your bag for emergencies. If you use a towel and/or grip sack, particularly as part of your pre-shot routine, consider keeping an extra one of each on hand in your bag in case of loss during a tournament. In an emergency, the last thing you want is to hold up play with a trip to the pro shop, or worse, scavenging accessories from other bowlers.

What Is a Benchmark Reaction?

By definition, a benchmark is a standard against which you compare other similar things. In bowling, a benchmark reaction usually entails a medium hook and a medium amount of angularity at the breakpoint. A benchmark reaction also tends to be fairly versatile and can be manipulated easily by bowlers who can adjust speed, axis rotation, and/or loft.

- Benchmark balls tend to have symmetrical cores with lower RGs and medium to strong differentials.
- Often, benchmark reactions are created by solid reactive coverstocks that provide predictable motion and strong continuation downlane.

Some bowlers will have a benchmark ball with different attributes, such as an asymmetrical core and/or a hybrid coverstock. Regardless of the exact ball, the goal is to have a reaction that helps you see the lanes well and provides versatility. The benchmark ball is often the first one out of your bag.

Time to Check Your Grip

When was the last time you checked your fit? If it's been more than a few years, then you should have your hand evaluated by a certified pro shop professional. Here are a few more signs that it's time to check your grip:

- **Pain**: If bowling causes pain in your hand, wrist, or anywhere in your arm, it could be linked to a poor fit.
- **Injury**: If you've had an unrelated injury, but one that affects your ability to hold or roll the ball, a new grip could help compensate for any new physical issue you're having.
- **Change in finger size**: Whether from weight gain or loss, arthritis, or any other potential cause, if your fingers or joints have changed size, you'll need to have your fit adjusted.

If the Shoe Fits...

Bowling shoes are an often-overlooked item in a bowler's bag. However, they form a key part of the approach as the bowler's source of contact with the lane. Proper bowling shoes are important in helping create proper footwork and balance throughout the approach:

- Entry-level shoes feature slide soles on both feet and are an introductory step to bowlers having all of their own equipment. Most of these shoes will cost less than a full year of renting shoes, so even beginners will get immediate value.
- The next level of shoe will feature a shoe that slides and a shoe that does not. The shoe that provides traction is for "pushing" into the slide, to allow more forward momentum into the release. As bowlers improve and their game advances, this kind of shoe is highly recommended.
- Competitive bowlers encounter a variety of different kinds of lanes and approaches. With different textures and levels of friction, competitive bowlers need the ability to modify the slide through changeable soles and/or heels. Advanced players should invest in these higher-end shoes to get the most from their game.

Minimizing Grip Pressure

All bowlers want to have a strong and consistent release. One of the key elements to achieving a great release is using the right amount of grip pressure.

A good release should feel like the ball is releasing from the hand, not the hand letting go of the bowling ball. The less grip pressure you have, the easier this will be. Consider these three important points:

- **Check your grip**: A proper fit is the most important part of reducing grip pressure.
- **Grip the ball like a glass**: You hold a glass or bottle with just enough pressure to not let it fall. Do the same with your bowling ball.
- **Fix your timing problems**: Poor timing is a prime cause of excessive grip pressure.

Basics of Bowling Ball Coverstocks

Not all bowling balls are created equally, with differentiation in both the internal core and the coverstock materials. Here are some of the basic differences when discussing the veneer of a bowling ball:

- Bowling balls are divided into three basic categories of coverstock: reactive resin, urethane, and polyester (plastic).
- Polyester balls create the least hook. Urethane balls with modern cores create low to medium hook. Reactive resin balls offer the most variety with low to high hook potential.
- Reactive resin and urethane coverstocks are also often further divided into the following three sub-categories:
  - Solids: These tend to hook earlier and tend to have sanded finishes.
  - Pearls: These tend to have more back end reaction and often have polished finishes.
  - Hybrids: These are a mix of the two and tend to have reactions that are in between solids and pearls.

Basics of Bowling Ball Cores

Bowling ball cores come in many shapes and sizes, but they all feature some key variables that help determine the kind of reaction the ball wants to make:

- Radius of Gyration, or RG, is a measurement of how fast the core spins and generally helps determine how early the ball wants to hook.
- Differential refers to the flare potential and the capacity of the ball to hook.
- Intermediate differential, or mass bias, is a measurement of the core's asymmetry, with higher values generally associated with greater amounts of hook.

Generally speaking, as core performance increases, so does the ball's price point.

Understanding Surface Adjustments

Managing a bowling ball's surface is one of the most important tactical skills a bowler can have. Along with being able to physically manipulate ball speed, loft, and release parameters, competitive bowlers need to be able to adjust their surfaces when needed and when allowed by the rules.

The goal of managing your ball surface is to create a matchup between your game, the ball, and the bowling environment. While every ball comes out of the box at a predetermined surface texture, bowlers can and should change that surface as necessary to improve the ball's performance:

- A rougher texture will create an earlier hook and a smoother overall shape. On many conditions, this will result in more overall hook.
- A smoother texture will create later hook and a sharper movement at the breakpoint. Adjust to a smoother surface when the ball is burning up too much energy too soon as it goes downlane.
- Not every ball reacts the same way to the same adjustment. Practice changing surfaces with all your equipment and take note of the differences in motion you see.

Bowling Ball Layouts

Layouts form a fundamental piece of ball motion. While surface accounts for more of the on-lane reaction, layouts determine what the ball "wants" to do—and layouts can't be changed to adapt to conditions like ball surface. For this reason, it's important to have some variety in the types of layouts you have in your bowling balls.

Keep these basic characteristics in mind when discussing layouts with your ball driller, or when deciding which ball to throw in competition:

- Higher pin positions have lower VAL angles or pin buffers, resulting in a sharper downlane motion; the opposite is true for lower pins.
- For asymmetrical balls, a mass bias indicator farther from the thumb creates a stronger, earlier hooking motion; placing it close to the thumb or in the track results in a weaker motion.

Remember that all of your layouts should be based on your positive axis point, or PAP, which your ball driller can determine.

Improving Your Thumb Exit

A strong and consistent release depends upon the thumb exiting the ball cleanly before the fingers impart the rotation and revolutions.

At some point, all bowlers can struggle with their feel and getting the ball off their thumb cleanly. Here are some tips to improve your thumb exit:

- **Check your fit**: Spans that are too long or too short and hole sizes that are the wrong shape or angle will impede your thumb exit and negatively impact your release.
- **Keep your thumbnail back**: Feeling your thumbnail against the back of the hole will ensure that you're not squeezing and will help you get your thumb out consistently.
- **Use tape**: Your thumb will change sizes slightly as you bowl, so be prepared to remove or add tape as necessary to maintain a consistent fit.

SECTION 3

LANE PLAY

Lane play consists of all the decisions a bowler must make to ensure the bowling ball gets to the pocket and strikes. Consistently getting strikes requires the right angle and optimal deflection through the pins.

There are four oil pattern variables that bowlers should pay most attention to. They are pattern length, oil volume, side-to-side ratio, and lengthwise taper. Let's take a quick look at each variable in more detail:

- **Pattern length and oil volume** will typically influence the area of the lane being played and the type and surface finish of the equipment you will likely need to use.

- **Side-to-side ratio** relates to the distribution of oil in the middle of the lane compared to the outside portion of the lane.
- **Lengthwise taper** refers to the distribution of oil from the front of the pattern compared to the end of the pattern.

Considering that the oil on the lane is moving and being removed with every shot thrown, the ideal ball path for each bowler is changing constantly over the course of a game or series of games.

Historically, bowling has always had an environment that changed due to the equipment going down the lane. However, modern equipment is more absorbent, and the oil on the lanes is affected more than ever before.

"Transition" is the accepted term for how the oil moves on the lane throughout a block of bowling, and it's this challenge that makes bowling unique. Few sports have competitive surfaces that change so much during competition.

In some cases, these changes are subtle, with little adjustment needed. In other cases, the required adjustments are more drastic, such as changing bowling balls or altering your release.

Bowlers at the top of the game are experts not just in the execution of their delivery, but also in "seeing" and adjusting to this transition. Effective lane play strategy is as much about mitigating the effects of transition as it is about effectively adjusting to what is in front of you.

Strategies for House Shots

A "typical house shot" is an oil pattern where there is a concentration of oil in the middle of the lane, with dry boards to the outside. They feature a higher side-to-side ratio, usually with more than 10 times the oil in the middle than on the outside.

While there can be variety in terms of how the pattern is laid out, there are some general rules of thumb when bowling on house shots:

- The large concentration of oil in the middle should be used as "hold" area. You want to play where you can still hit the pocket on misses to the inside.
- The drier boards outside are a "recovery" zone. You want to play where misses to the outside can hook back to the pocket.
- Even bowlers with a lower hook potential style can benefit from playing near this "oil line" where the concentration of oil drops significantly, usually somewhere between the first and second arrows.
- Bowlers with larger hooks will generally want to lay the ball down in the heavier concentration area and send the ball out toward the drier boards.

Strategies for Sport Shots

"Sport shots" feature a flatter application of the oil on the lane, which creates less room or area for the bowler to hit and still get the ball to the pocket. While the strategy will differ for the various lengths and volumes, there are some basic guidelines for getting started on these kinds of patterns:

- Bowlers will want to start with straighter angles compared to house shots. Without as much recovery to the outside, it's generally better to use a more direct line compared to what you would use on a house shot.
- When the length of the pattern is known, a good general guide is to use the "Rule of 31" where you subtract 31 from the pattern length to get an idea of where you want the ball to be downlane. For example, a pattern that is 38 feet long will yield a result of seven, meaning that you'll want the ball to be near the seven board at the end of the pattern.
- This is less of a tactical tip than a mental one, but patience is key for bowling on challenging conditions. The strikes won't come as easily, so bowlers need to be patient and make their spares.

Attacking Fresh Oil

Regardless of the type of pattern being used, fresh oil offers unique characteristics, including dry back ends and the heaviest concentration of oil in the heads compared to when transition has taken place.

Getting out of the gates with a good first game can be the key to a successful league night or tournament. Relative to what you'll find yourself doing later in the block, a good fresh oil strategy often includes the following:

- **Smoother ball motion**: Fresh oil features the quickest transition from oil to dry at the end of the pattern, so your first ball will likely be the smoothest in shape that you'll use that day.
- **More surface**: This goes hand-in-hand with smoother motions. Using a rougher surface texture compared to balls later in the block provides more control and easier transition.
- **Straighter angles**: Not every pattern will be played perfectly straight, but you want to start straighter to help manage transition and keep from getting way too deep way too early.

Practicing Surface Adjustments

The best way to improve any skill is to practice it. Spending time in a practice session with your bowling balls and some abrasive pads is a great investment for better understanding your equipment and improving your lane play skills:

- Pick a ball and make note of its starting surface before you begin. Sand the entire surface with a 500 grit pad. Throw a few shots to note how much hook you see and where the ball starts to hook.
- Repeat this process for each pad and each bowling ball to see how they respond to the different surfaces.
- Any surface adjustment you make can be undone and changed back to the starting surface. Note that a pro shop or ball spinner will likely be required to return a ball to a shiny polished finish.

The "Three P's" of Lane Play

Everyone wants to make better decisions out on the lanes. When it comes down to it, good lane play really comes down to these three things:

- **Perceive**: Watch every aspect of your ball's motion from the time it hits the lane to the time it goes off the back of the pin deck. Pay attention to how the pins and ball deflect.
- **Process**: Analyze the information to decide if you need an adjustment and to determine what to do. With experience, this can be done unconsciously. When you're confused, make sure you take the time you need to consciously process the available information.
- **Perform**: Once you've made a decision, commit to your desired plan and simply execute the shot.

Understanding Lane Surfaces

Lane surface type and its level of wear and tear will affect how much friction you see, while topography will also impact how much a ball hooks. These details become even more important on flatter conditions and can drastically impact your strategy.

- Older lanes will have more friction up front. Use weaker layouts, less surface, and/or higher degrees of axis rotation or tilt to help the ball retain energy for the back end.
- No lane is perfectly flat, and each one is unique. Additional hook or a hang spot downlane is often the result of topography. Use speed and angle adjustments to adjust and get back in the pocket.
- Lanes tilted away from the gutters will provide more forgiveness than those tilted toward the gutters. Use tighter angles if you see hang outside of the five board, even on shorter/drier patterns.

Dealing With Carrydown

Carrydown diminishes the back end reaction of a bowling ball due to oil being deposited downlane. While you can opt to change balls or adjust your angles, you can also make some small physical adjustments to your release to help find the right reaction:

- **Slow down**: Reducing your speed not only gives the ball more time to hook, but it also creates a more defined breakpoint shape relative to higher ball speeds. This is exactly what you need when facing carrydown.
- **Increase axis rotation**: Increasing your degree of axis rotation will help increase your ball's back end hook to counteract the diminishing downlane friction from carrydown.

Used alone or in combination with an equipment change or line change, these physical adjustments can help counter the effects of carrydown on the lanes.

Target Line Adjustments

One of the most basic adjustments that a bowler can make is a target line adjustment. This involves adjusting the foot position, the target, or both to change the line and angle of the ball as it is delivered.

Target line adjustments are generally referred to by two numbers, such as a 2-and-1 or a 2-and-2:

- The first number refers to the number of boards that the bowler moves their starting position.
- The second number refers to the number of boards the bowler moves their target on the lane.

For example, if a bowler makes a 2-and-1 adjustment to the inside, they move their feet 2 boards in and their target 1 board in.

Line adjustments are used to change the amount of oil the ball encounters on the lane by changing where it is placed to find more or less oil, based on how much the ball is hooking. Understanding this basic system is key for any beginner or intermediate player, and especially for those bowling on teams so they can communicate their adjustments to their teammates.

Warming Up for Tournaments

Even if you are bowling in a center where you've competed before and have an idea of what the oil pattern will be, the process of warming up for a tournament is a bit different from warming up for league.

You still need a dynamic warm-up prior to throwing your first ball, but you also need a strategy for finding a good line by the end of practice:

- **Start with your benchmark ball**: This is a ball with a smoother shape and a medium hook to help you narrow down your options to start.
- **Start with straighter angles**: Test lines up the first and second arrows to get a sense for where there is some hold on the lanes.
- **Find the hook**: Open your angles slightly to see where you can find recovery, and then refine your line and ball choice based on everything you've seen.

Tips for Short Oil

Sport patterns can be very challenging, due to the extra oil toward the outside of the lane and the smaller margin for error. Shorter oil can be especially challenging for bowlers who are used to having plenty of oil in the middle of the lane.

When faced with shorter oil, here are a few general suggestions to help you control your ball reaction and stay in the pocket:

- Use more forward roll so the ball reacts less violently to the back end.
- Target a breakpoint that is closer to the gutter and not as far downlane.
- Bowl with smoother-reacting balls, like urethanes or lower-flaring reactives.

Tips for Medium Oil

Medium-length sport patterns have the most possible variety in them, due to a less defined initial strategy compared to longer or shorter patterns. But bowlers don't just need to react to what's out there. Here are a few tips to help with your game plan:

- **Straighter is greater**: Start with smoother, less aggressive balls to control the breakpoint on the fresh.
- **Forget the house shot**: On the fresh, the more you move inside, the more hook you tend to find, not less. If you're going high, move farther outside. When going light, go farther inside.
- **Manage transition**: Stick to smoother shapes as long as possible to keep transition easier to see and manage. Weak pocket hits are better than splits through the nose.

Tips for Longer Oil

Longer oil sport patterns can be difficult for bowlers with lower rev rates, or those who are used to playing open angles toward the gutter.

When faced with longer oil, here are a few tips to help you find good ball reaction and stay in the pocket:

- Keep your angles straighter on the fresh. Use a breakpoint closer to the headpin and farther downlane.
- Use stronger balls that are drilled to finish strong, not roll early. Sand the balls to create enough friction in the midlane.
- Be prepared to adjust quickly. The prevalence of stronger, sanded balls will dry out the pattern faster than what you normally see on house shots or shorter oil.

Adjusting to High-Pocket Hits

Not all high hits are created equal. Why does one player go high and trip the 4 pin when your shot does not? It's all about angles and ball reaction.

Here's what to do the next time you're faced with these common high-pocket leaves:

- **9 pin**: This isn't technically a high hit, so much as a pocket hit with too much angle. Look for a smoother shape that will deflect through the pins properly.
- **4 pin**: This is generally a high hit, but it also trips out with the right ball reaction. An earlier, smoother motion (think more surface) might need to be combined with a move on the lane to solve this problem.
- **3 pin**: Any combination of a 3 pin is a sign of too much hook, and possibly a ball that is over-responding to the back end. Start by reducing the hook and then work on smoothing out the shape, if necessary.

When to Adjust Axis Rotation Angle

You've worked on your game, and you can now manipulate your release to increase or decrease your axis rotation. How do you know when to use this skill?

The degree of axis rotation is a fundamental piece of your release that dictates hook potential. Being able to manipulate your release to change how much rotation you apply affects the shape of your ball motion and can be used in different situations:

- Increasing your degree of axis rotation will usually increase back end motion, with all other things being equal. This is generally most effective as lanes break down, when playing open angles, or when you are seeing a lack of back end movement.
- Decreasing your degree of axis rotation has the opposite effect. This is best used on fresher, flatter conditions, shorter oil, and when playing straighter angles—essentially any time you want to minimize hook and maximize control.

Identifying Transition

Transition is the specific combination of oil carrydown and oil breakdown. How much you see and where it happens on the lane are different every time we bowl, but here are things to look for to help you better "see" the lane oil moving around:

- Good shots where the ball grabs early and miss the breakpoint to the inside or roll out early are an indication of breakdown in the heads.
- Balls that seem to hook, then slide, then hook again are a good indication of breakdown and plenty of carrydown.
- When duller balls have not rolled by the time they get to the pocket, there is probably more carrydown than breakdown.

Battling Dry Lanes

There are many ways for a lane to be "dry," and they don't all require the same strategy for getting your ball back in the pocket. Here are the most common issues that bowlers will face when it comes to dry lanes:

- **Transition**: Oil is removed as shots are thrown. You will need to find more oil or make choices that reduce hook, such as changing to a weaker ball or increasing ball speed.
- **Lane surface**: Older synthetic panels and wood lanes offer more friction. Choose balls and skills that delay hook, such as weaker layouts or spinning the ball more.
- **Oil pattern**: Shorter oil offers a lot of friction at the back of the lane. In this case, you want to reduce hook and use a smoother shape. Examples of how this can be achieved are to use urethane equipment or more forward roll.

Observe, Accept, Adjust

When it comes to lane play, every bowler wants to improve. Whether you're a beginner or an advanced player, once you understand the value of making good adjustments, you always want to make them better and faster.

The ability to make good adjustments depends on three essential steps: observe, accept, and adjust.

- **Observe**: Watch the ball as it goes down the lane to observe the shape and amount of hook, and then watch the pins to get clues about your deflection. Also, pay attention to other bowlers on your lane to learn even more about the conditions.
- **Accept**: Easier said than done, bowlers should accept what they see in front of them, rather than blame themselves for a bad shot.
- **Adjust**: Once you've observed and accepted, simply make the move based on what you see. From physical manipulation to ball changes or angle changes, you can't do this well unless you've done the first two steps.

All Lanes Are Different

Not all bowling lanes are created equal. While bowlers generally understand that the oil can drastically influence their lane play strategies, the pattern is only one part of the environment.

The lane's topography and friction characteristics can vary from lane to lane and make each of the lanes in a center play very differently:

- The most-used lanes in the house have the highest amount of friction and tend to hook more. Be ready for more hook on lanes that get assigned first for league and open play.
- Topography can make a drastic difference. Trust your eyes if you throw the ball well and it doesn't react as you expected, as topography may be to blame.
- Even on house shots, it's best to assume that the two lanes on a pair are different. Just because you make a move on the right lane, that doesn't mean you need to make the same move on the left lane.

Pin Carry and the Role of Deflection

At its simplest, strikes are the result of appropriate deflection of the ball as it hits the pins. Too much deflection or too little deflection will create the wrong angles for the pins to deflect into each other. In these cases, the solution is to find a way to change your ball reaction to create more optimal deflection through the pins.

Too much deflection often results in flat 10 pins and "weak" splits, such as the 8/10 (for righthanders). Here, bowlers need to create less deflection by going to a ball that retains energy longer, increasing their axis rotation angle, and generally delaying the ball's hook.

Too little deflection will often result in 9 pins or ringing 10 pins. To create more deflection, try to get the ball to roll a bit sooner and/or skid a bit less by using more forward roll or more surface, or by switching to a less angular bowling ball.

Breakdown Versus Carrydown

Transition consists of a combination of oil breakdown and oil carrydown. The relative amounts of breakdown and carrydown will vary, due mostly to the size and characteristics of the field, the lines being played, and the type of equipment being used.

Breakdown occurs when oil is removed from the lane. This happens most with sanded, high-flaring reactive resin balls that pull the oil off the lane with each shot. Expect to move inside quickly or change to weaker equipment when many of these balls are in play, particularly when the field's rev rate is high.

Carrydown refers to oil being dragged downlane by the bowling ball as it exits the oil pattern. This happens most with low-flaring, less absorbent balls such as polyester or urethane, but reactive resin balls can also create carrydown. Expect the lanes to get tighter downlane in a field with lots of urethane in play, or in a field with more low rev rate bowlers.

Exploring an Unknown Oil Pattern

Tournament bowlers are often bowling on an unknown condition. The key to adjusting to an unknown environment is using every shot in practice to collect information, even though the first few won't be at full power.

Use your benchmark ball to explore an unknown condition and then adjust accordingly:

- Your first couple of shots can be used to determine the pattern length by looking for where the ball hooks sharply when it exits the pattern. This is easier to see at lower ball speeds.
- As you get closer to your normal release potential, learn about the overall friction levels by opening your angles slightly to test the outside, and then closing them slightly to test the hold.
- With these two pieces of information, and now that you're fully loosened up, you can approximate the desired area of play and determine if your benchmark ball's reaction is appropriate. If necessary, change balls. Then adjust the coverstock surface, if the rules allow.

Adjusting to Light Pocket Hits

Hitting light in the pocket doesn't usually result in strikes. Whether from an errant shot or a good shot, if you hit light in the pocket, the various 2-pin combination leaves (for righthanders) aren't all created equal.

In addition to not quite hitting enough of the headpin, the different pin combinations left standing give hints about your ball reaction:

- **2/4/5**: Bucket combinations (with or without the 8 pin), usually occur when the ball is rolling out and losing energy too early.
- **2/8**: When the 5 pin goes down and you leave something like a 2/8, 2/8/10, or 2/4/8, the ball is likely not finishing its hook phase early enough.
- **2 pin alone**: When this pin stands alone, you likely have the right overall reaction shape that was simply thrown off-line or is in need of a small angle change.

Pay attention to your light-pocket leaves and you won't need to wait for a better shot, or more information, in order to adjust accordingly and get back to striking.

Making the Wrong Adjustment

Every bowler has been faced with the situation of needing to make an adjustment, being unsure what to do, and then picking the wrong one. In these situations, what's the best course of action?

A lane play decision is always an educated guess. The higher your experience level and the more skills you have, the more likely you will be to pick the right adjustment, but we all make mistakes. When you realize you've made a wrong choice, here's what to do.

Just breathe. What's done is done, so beating yourself up about it doesn't help in the moment. A wrong adjustment is simply an option crossed off your list, so go back to the options you considered before. You've learned something, so move forward and commit to the next adjustment, rather than dwelling on the mistake.

Solving Corner Pin Problems

Leaving corner pins can be frustrating. However, if you're paying close enough attention, the way in which the pin remains standing can tell you what you need to do about it to get back to striking:

- A solid 10, also known as a wrap 10, occurs when the 6 pin flies right around the 10 pin. This is often a sign that the ball is entering the pocket a bit too aggressively and you should look for a slightly smoother motion.
- A flat 10 occurs when the 6 pin just falls into the gutter. This is often a sign that the ball is losing too much energy going down the lane and you need to find a sharper reaction or look for a bit more oil to help the ball retain more energy.

Adjusting Your Breakpoint

Many bowlers today are familiar with the "Rule of 31." By taking the pattern length in feet and subtracting 31, you get a general starting point guideline for which board your ball should be on when it exits the oil pattern. But what about optimal breakpoint distance? This also tends to vary with oil pattern length.

While most bowlers are able to move their eyes from board to board when they target, they must also be capable of adjusting their breakpoint distances:

- For shorter oil, you not only generally want your breakpoint to be closer to the gutter, but you also want it a little closer to the foul line.
- For longer oil, you generally want your breakpoint farther inside, but also closer to the pins.

Solving for Flat Hits

Corner pins are often the result of too much deflection when the ball hits the pocket. Many bowlers have a favorite adjustment for those pesky corner pins, but when that doesn't work, or if you're not sure what to do, there are plenty of other options that can be effective, depending on your style and preferences.

Consider one of these options to reduce deflection when you need to improve your pin carry:

- Create a sharper back end reaction by using a more angular ball or by adjusting your hand position.
- Use more of the headpin by hitting a little higher in the pocket.
- Change your angle by making a small adjustment with your feet, without moving your target.

Understanding Lane Surface Types

Take the time to get to know the lanes you bowl on. Make note of what seems to work most often and be ready to select your tournament arsenal based on the lane surface tendencies that you become aware of at each of the centers where you compete.

- **Wood**: Highest friction, often old and well-worn, with a defined track area. High ball speeds, higher tilt, and higher axis rotation can help to get balls through the lane with enough pop to carry.
- **AMF synthetics**: Generally lower friction than wood and higher friction than Brunswick synthetics, usually favoring balls that retain energy for the back end.
- **Brunswick synthetics**: Newer lanes are generally lower friction, favoring stronger covers. Older lanes can be very high friction in the fronts, affecting lane play decisions and ball selection to get the ball through the heads.

Old Lanes Versus New Lanes

Bowling in an older center that has more lane wear? This increases the friction of any type of lane, whether wood or synthetic.

On older lanes, you'll probably need weaker equipment, later-hooking layouts, and/or a smoother, shinier surface to help the ball get down the lane.

The opposite is generally true when bowling in a newer center that has less lane wear.

As always with lane play suggestions, **let your ball be your guide**. Don't let preconceptions about the condition of the lane surface affect your decisions during competition.

Improving Lane Play Decisions

When you are faced with a lane play decision and you're unsure what to do, pick the option that you have the most confidence in executing properly and then **commit to it**.

When you're not fully committed to your decision, even the right lane play choice will yield worse execution and increase the likelihood of a bad result.

To quote a famous mentor from another galaxy, "Do or do not. There is no try."

Recognizing Scoring Patterns

Have you noticed a scoring trend in your league or tournament play? Do you always start slowly and finish strong? Or get off to a hot start and then slow down? Maybe the second game is always your worst game?

While there can be any number of explanations, the first step is to become aware of your scoring patterns to figure out how to address them:

- Do you often struggle at the end of a block? This could be from physical or mental fatigue, so examine your behavior in the 24 hours leading up to the tournament.

- Do you usually start slow and finish strong? This could be a matter of a lack of focus and intensity prior to starting a block. Create or modify your pre-competition routine to help get you energized before a tournament.

- Is one of your league games consistently the lowest? First, make sure that this is factual and not just perception by checking the data. Then address potential reasons such as focus, energy, or being slow to recognize or make adjustments.

SECTION 4

THE MENTAL GAME

The principles of sport psychology have become important across all of sports, and bowling is no different. Competing at the highest level requires a very solid mental game, but even beginners can benefit from a good mindset.

Understanding the difference between performance and outcome, the basics of good breathing and focus, advanced concepts like thought-stopping, and the various uses of visualization are all mental game topics that can benefit all bowlers.

One of the key mental game elements in the sport of bowling is the pre-shot routine, a concept that is well-known in the golf world. Many of the similarities that bowling draws from golf are on the mental side of things.

Both feature a relatively short execution phase of the swing or approach followed by a relatively long pause before executing again. During this time, many negative or distracting thoughts can creep in, so it's here where a strong mental game forms the foundation of good performance.

The pre-shot routine forms the transition phase from being distracted and socializing to refocusing on your execution and the "task at hand," which is to roll the ball as well as you can.

Aside from the frame to frame needs that a bowler has, the mental game is also important from a macro point of view to avoid slumps and to get out of them when they happen.

Managing the ups and downs of competition, not to mention your skill development, is a key part of consistently performing well. Again, mental skills such as goal setting and keeping perspective become very important.

Historically, the mental game might have been ignored, but not so anymore. If you want to improve at any sport, and especially a precision sport like bowling, you need to develop your mental skills just as much, if not more, than your physical skills.

Luckily, many of these skills can be developed away from the lanes, as well as during practice sessions, so all it takes is some commitment and time to learn some valuable mental tools that can elevate your bowling game.

Managing Expectations

What level of expectations should a bowler have about their next tournament? It's fine to have high hopes, but what can they really expect? Much like goals, this depends on the specific type of expectation you set for yourself.

Results-based expectations can cause anxiety if they are higher than a bowler really believes they can achieve. On the other hand, lower expectations about the results can free up the mind to stay in the present and focus on performance.

Performance-based expectations are different. They are about a bowler holding themselves accountable to a high standard of execution, making good decisions, and using their mental tools effectively. In short, having high expectations for yourself is about controlling what you can control. No one is perfect, but you try to live up to high performance ideals.

The Basics of Self-Talk

The way we talk to ourselves—even in our heads—can influence our current and future bowling performances. Here are some simple tips for helping you improve your self-talk on the lanes:

- Avoid using the word "should" (i.e., "I should have known I'd choke and miss the cut!").
- Use statements of intent instead of statements of avoidance. For example, "stop muscling the ball" is a statement of avoidance that describes what you want to *stop* doing. It is far better to describe what you *intend* to do, such as "relaxed, free armswing."
- Talk to yourself the same way you would talk to a teammate.

Negative self-talk is a habit that initially requires conscious, deliberate effort to change. Be on the lookout for negative self-talk and make the decision to change your patterns for the better.

An Effective Pre-Shot Routine

Pre-shot routines vary tremendously among top-level players, but there are several common elements they share that you can incorporate into yours:

- Visualization, such as target or line.
- Positive self-talk.
- A repetitive motion, like wiping the ball or shoe.
- Very little time once "set" into the stance.

You can practice your pre-shot routine at home by writing it down and then practicing it up until the moment you take your first step. Then stop, put the ball down, take a small break for 10 to 30 seconds, and start the process over.

When to Take a Break

Rest is an important part of high-level performance, but many bowlers are reluctant to take breaks. Here are some signs that you should consider taking a few weeks off, or at least easing up your schedule:

- **Injury**: When minor nagging pains are affecting your day-to-day life and your performance out on the lanes, it's time to take a break and let those wounds heal up.
- **Mental lapses**: If you find yourself making more and more mental mistakes or losing your cool more often, it's a sign that you need a mental break from the competitive grind.
- **Poor execution**: When the body is physically worn out, it will be hard to execute at the proper level. Taking a complete rest or cutting back on the practice time can help the body recuperate so you can perform better when you return.

Visualizing Success

If seeing is believing, then being able to see yourself achieve success is an important factor in believing you can do it. With this in mind, visualization can be a key component in unlocking your potential.

For best results, try to do the following:

- **Just relax**: Close your eyes and use slow, deep breaths to be calm and focused as you begin your visualization.
- **Add details**: Include the voices of other bowlers, the smell of your bowling ball, and other details, along with your own successful execution.
- **Practice the skill**: It's not enough to simply use imagery while competing. Rehearse and practice your imagery away from the lanes or as part of an on-lane practice session so you can improve its effectiveness.

Scoreboard-Watching

It's easy to say that bowlers should be in the moment, ignore the scoreboard, and focus on performance, but it's hard to do that in a tight match or when you know you need a big score to make the cut in a tournament.

Here are some tips on how you can look at the scoreboard and still be ready to throw your best shot each frame:

- **Shift your focus**: Between shots, it's normal to check the score. Use your pre-shot routine to refocus on internal cues and execution, rather than keeping an external focus on the score.
- **Breathe**: It's as simple as it gets. Taking a deep breath signals your brain that everything is okay and helps your system relax for a better shot.
- **Embrace the moment**: Being thankful for the opportunity to perform in the clutch will help take the pressure off. You'll be okay no matter the outcome, so try to enjoy it.

Reframing Distraction

Reframing is the process of changing your perspective on a given situation by viewing it through a more positive lens. Almost anything can be reframed into a positive or neutral context, rather than a negative one, which can help you keep a strong mindset on the lanes.

For example, when faced with a lane breakdown that causes a delay or even a change in pairs, bowlers can reframe this scenario into an opportunity to thrive. Use your mental skills to stay focused. In the case of a lane change, frame this as an opportunity to use your lane play skills to adapt quickly.

When faced with a tough pattern or unexpected ball reaction, many bowlers become confused and defeated. Reframing this kind of tough environment into an enjoyable test, and one that everyone must cope with, can help take the pressure off and ease your mind and your swing to find a solution.

Pre-Tournament Routines

To get into the right mindset before practice even starts, it helps to have a routine before league or tournament play begins. Elite athletes have routines that start 24 hours or more before game time, but to get started, just focus on the following pre-competition elements:

- Arrive with enough time to comfortably get ready to bowl, allowing time for things like registering for the tournament and putting on your skin patch.
- Do things in a consistent order and try to do them in a similar place each time. For example, always tying your shoes last, right before practice starts, at the back of the settee area. Details matter to help normalize unfamiliar environments.
- Pick a time to do some visualization to get into the right mindset. This can be with the ball and line you plan to start with, or you can simply replay past successes in your mind's eye.

Reviewing Your Season

When your bowling season ends, it's important to spend time reviewing your performance, especially if you set goals at the outset. Did you achieve those goals?

It's one of many questions you can pose to help you decide your course of action in the off-season. Here are a few more:

- What aspect(s) of your game improved this year? Where did you underperform?
- Did your practice support your goals? Do you need to practice more, or practice differently?
- Did your league bowling support your tournament bowling? Was it too much or not enough?
- Are you committed to another season? What are your goals for next year?

This process is important at both the end of one season and the beginning of another to remind yourself of your intentions, or to adjust your goals if things have changed.

The Value of a Deep Breath

Ever wonder why a few deep breaths can have such a huge influence on performance? When a bowler is feeling pressure, the sympathetic nervous system kicks into high gear, triggering the famous "fight or flight" response.

This increases tension in the body, which is counterproductive to an effective release. Even a single deep breath can counteract this tension, as it lets the body know that everything is okay.

Incorporate at least one deep breath into your pre-shot routine, either while waiting to step onto the approach or as you assume your starting position, to help relax your mind and body. The breath should be fairly long and slow; allow your belly to expand, and don't raise your shoulders. This triggers a more relaxed state, helping improve your chances of coming through under pressure.

The Basics of Setting Goals

Bowlers often set goals such as attaining a higher average or making more cuts in tournaments. However, outcome-oriented goals such as these should not be the end of the goal-setting process.

To set performance or process goals, simply ask yourself "How?" once you've set an outcome goal. For each outcome goal, try to set at least three process goals which are steps toward achieving that goal.

Here is an example:

Outcome goal: Achieve a 200 average.

How?

- Improve single pin spare shooting to 90 percent.
- Find a coach and straighten my swing to be more consistent.
- Replace my older equipment and double-check my fit.

Improving Your Pre-Shot Routine

The pre-shot routine is a fairly well-known mental tool that most high-level bowlers use to improve their performance. From a simple deep breath to a multi-step process, each one is unique.

Once you've formed the base of your pre-shot routine, or even if you are just forming it, here are some helpful tips to improve the effectiveness of each step:

- When visualizing your shot, always include the ball going through the pins for a strike, not simply hitting your target at the arrows.
- When using self-talk, use the first person and say, "I've got this," rather than, "You've got this."
- Use a trigger, such as tapping the ball, to establish a rhythm in your stance that will match the rhythm of the approach.
- Remember to breathe at the same rate whether you are in a pressure situation or are completely relaxed. Focus on slower, deeper breaths to center yourself before starting the approach.

Reviewing Your League Night

There is immense value in debriefing a tournament with a coach, but not everyone can do this, and bowlers bowl leagues more often than tournaments. To help make the most of your league nights, here is a way to reflect on each night as you head home from the center.

Spend some time thinking about three things you'd like to do better, such as a single bad shot or a missed adjustment. Limit this to only the three items, even on bad nights when the list can be longer.

Next, reflect on at least three things you did well and are proud of. This can even be making a single pin to break a string of opens, or a strong finish to save a game.

Finally, commit to repeating the good things next week. Plan to practice the other areas, or to improve your performance of them in your next league night.

Performing Under Pressure

Every bowler wants to be able to come through in the clutch. Whether it's a key spare or a double in the tenth frame, we all want to perform when we really need it.

Performing in pressure situations is all about mindset. You want to normalize the situation as much as possible, while still acknowledging the moment. Here are some tips to improve your execution in the clutch:

- Perform your pre-shot routine as usual. Many bowlers try to slow down too much, affecting their tempo and giving them more time to think. Maintain your usual pace from the time the arrow is up to the delivery of the ball.
- You must want to perform well and not be afraid to get a bad result. It's an important distinction, and one that separates bowlers who come through in the clutch from those who don't.
- Embrace the nerves. It's normal to have a few butterflies. Embrace them as a sign that you are doing what you love, competing on the lanes, rather than trying to ignore them or push them down.

Understand Locus of Control

Are you in control of whether you get a strike? Not really. Understanding what's in your control versus what's not can help bring perspective to your game.

There are plenty of things you can't control that affect your bowling game: where everyone else is playing and the equipment they use, pins that might be off spot, the pace of play, the lane conditions themselves, and lots of other factors.

Recognizing these elements that affect you and accepting that they are beyond your control will lead to a better perspective than becoming frustrated.

As a bowler, you are in control of the decisions you make, the focus you bring and where you place it, your mental game, and your execution. Your goal should be to maximize these areas and simply accept the things you can't control.

Control and Acceptance

The phrase "control what you can control" is fairly common in coaching these days, but it can often leave bowlers a bit confused about what exactly it means.

An effective mental game and good lane play require the ability to address the things within our control and accept and adapt to the things that aren't.

As a bowler, the things within your control include your mental response to a bad break, your self-talk, your ball choices and lane play decisions, and also the routines you use and the mindset you adopt before you step into the bowling center.

The most important thing you must accept that is beyond your control is the ball's reaction once it leaves your hand. Other things outside your control include the lane play strategies of people on your pair, lane breakdowns and scheduling issues, and the format of the tournament, all of which can become unnecessary distractions that negatively affect your on-lane performance.

Refining Your Bowling Self-Talk

Self-talk is the mind's internal dialogue. It can be either positive or negative, and it can either be a fantastic mental tool or a burden of self-defeating chatter.

In addition to the benefits of trying to talk to yourself in a generally positive way, bowlers can refine their self-talk with a few important details, and by using self-talk purposefully in their routines:

- Incorporate personal statements into your pre-shot routine. These can be meaningful quotes or your own positive affirmations.
- When using positive affirmations, speak to yourself in the first person: for example, say, "I can do this," rather than, "You can do this."
- When trying to cut off negative thoughts, use the third-person perspective as a distancing technique by using your name. For example, say, "Okay, John…just take a breath."

Outcome Orientation Versus Process Orientation

Where is your focus while you are bowling? Is it on the score, the execution of the next shot, or something else? Whether you are outcome-oriented or process-oriented can have a dramatic impact on your performance.

Outcome orientation is having a focus on the result. In bowling, that can be the result of getting a strike each frame, the final score, or making a cut in a tournament. It is natural for people to want to accomplish the object of the game, but, unfortunately, this can cause some anxiety. Bowlers can benefit by instead keeping their focus on how to achieve the desired result, which is otherwise known as process orientation.

Focusing on the process means keeping your focus on each task that makes up a good shot. Focusing on process items—like the pre-shot routine, observing ball reaction, and making good adjustments—is what eventually results in more strikes, higher scores, and making more cuts.

Managing Your Intensity Level

Maintaining an optimum level of intensity throughout a tournament block is a key element of optimizing your performance. Bowlers who experience changes in their intensity level during competition can use some simple tricks to help manage that.

If you want to start stronger, or be more consistent throughout a tournament block, use these tips to help you get to and stay at your optimum intensity:

- **Listen to music (or sing it in your head)**: If you're extra nervous or amped up, listen to something soothing. If you're a little flat, listen to something more up-tempo.
- **Use your breathing**: Long, slow breaths can calm you down, but you can also choose slightly shorter, shallower breaths to get you into a more intense mode.
- **Adjust your warm-up**: Pace your warm-up routine, from tying your shoes to performing dynamic stretches, to match your desired intensity level.

The Basics of a Competition Debrief

Experience is considered to be a great teacher, but learning from your experiences requires some reflection. Bowlers can and should debrief themselves following any competitive event, including leagues or tournament play.

From league play to a PBA major, any level of competition can offer insights for a bowler, regardless of the quality of the performance. If you want to learn from both the positives and the negatives of a competition experience, you can debrief yourself, preferably in a journal, by asking the following questions:

- Did I achieve my goals, surpass them, or fall short? Where is the gap?
- Where did my performance fall short? How can I improve next time?
- What went well that I wish to repeat? What are the bright spots that I can pull out of a sub-par performance?

What's Your Process?

We often hear pros talk about "sticking with the process." Whether they are referring to the process of working on their physical games or staying within their game plans during competition, having a personal process is key to achieving success on the lanes.

When professional bowlers talk about their "process," they're usually referring to the collections of routines they use to navigate a competition block. This can start as early as the night before the tournament starts, but it generally includes everything from the overall game plan to the pre-shot routine:

- A pre-competition routine sets your intention for the block, including your intended game plan, your overall mindset, and your plan for managing your intensity level.
- The shot cycle includes the pre-shot routine, the execution itself, and the reaction to the result.
- The process also includes the routine between shots, including whether you stand or sit, how social you are, and other personal elements that can affect your performance.

Rebuilding Your Confidence

Every athlete in every sport can face confidence issues, and bowlers are no exception. Regardless of your skill level, confidence plays a major role in helping you perform up to your potential.

Confidence exists on a spectrum. It can be high or low, and it often moves back and forth between the two based on recent results, practice sessions, or even off-lane influences such as work. For bowlers struggling with confidence, here are a few ways to help give it a boost:

- **Focus on positive self-talk**: Be aware of negative thoughts and shift your perspective onto what you want to do, rather than what you're afraid of.
- **Remember past success**: When slumping, it's easy to forget the good times, so make a mental list and relive some of your best moments as a reminder of your best self.
- **Be patient**: Confidence won't instantly climb out of the gutter like magic. Rushing the process is a sure-fire way to trigger more negative thoughts.

Setting Performance Goals

Have you set bowling goals? If so, the odds are good that most of your goals are outcome-related, such as achieving a certain average or winning a tournament. While these are important goals to set, bowlers need another type of goal to help them on their journey.

Performance goals are also called process goals because they focus on the steps you need to take in order to achieve a certain outcome. For example, improving your spare shooting is a performance goal. To be effective, performance goals should be precise, such as, "Improve single-pin conversion percentage to a 90% success rate."

When setting goals, start with your desired outcomes (i.e., winning a tournament) and then ask yourself, "How?" as many times as necessary to find the main performance goals you can use as benchmarks on your journey to success.

We Are What We Think We Are

How you see yourself as a bowler has a huge influence on your performance. While most bowlers try to view their games in a positive light, sometimes the way we describe ourselves can be limiting and we don't even know it.

How do you describe yourself as a bowler? For example, do you describe yourself as a grinder? While this term is often viewed as a positive, indicating mental toughness, it can also hold you back. By definition, grinders don't get many long strings of strikes, so maybe you struggle to strike enough because that's not a fit with how you view your game.

Think of three words that describe yourself as a bowler, and then consider both the positive and potential negative impacts that they might have on your game. By being aware of some of these self-limiting implications, we can shift our thinking to match who we want to be out on the lanes.

Pre-Shot Routine Visualization

Visualization is one of the most important elements of the pre-shot routine, but its function isn't simply to pre-play the shot you're about to throw.

Rather, it serves to move you out of your analytical mind and into the visual/performance part of your brain. In order to do this, the visualization must be as detailed as possible.

Effective use of imagery in the pre-shot routine will help eliminate internal distractions by giving you a clear picture of the shot you are trying to execute. As part of your pre-shot routine, try to incorporate visualization that includes:

- A first-person perspective.
- A key feeling from the approach (i.e., an effortless swing).
- The intended ball path and result.

Thought-Stopping Techniques

Having a hard time shutting down negative thoughts while bowling? Consider using a thought-stopping technique.

Thought-stopping is a type of visualization exercise to help you actively put an end to negative thoughts and replace them with positive ones. It is essentially a two-step process. You first visualize something to call attention to the act of stopping, and then you use a pre-determined thought or idea to replace the negative thinking.

For example, when you catch yourself thinking negatively, you could do the following:

- Visualize a referee throwing a flag or blowing a whistle.
- Say, "I've got this!" while visualizing yourself executing flawlessly.

The Four Types of Focus

Lack of focus is often cited as an excuse for bad bowling, but focus is actually all about making sure you are paying attention to the right things at the right time.

There are four different kinds of focus we all use without knowing it, but we need to be aware of which one to use when the situation calls for it. We use the four types of focus all the time while bowling, almost in sequence. Understanding your focus strengths and weaknesses can help you address which parts you need to work on off the lanes.

Here are the four types of focus and when they are used in the shot cycle:

- **Broad/external**: Observing ball motion.
- **Broad/internal**: Contemplating adjustments.
- **Narrow/internal**: Pre-shot routine.
- **Narrow/external**: Targeting.

Watch What You Say

Visualization works because your mind doesn't know the difference between real and imagined experiences. This can also work in a negative way when you replay mistakes over and over again, regardless of whether you do it out loud to a friend or to yourself in your mind.

If you've missed a spare or had a bad break, one of the worst things you can do is talk about it to everyone that's willing to listen. By repeating the story of your mistake, you're replaying the events in your mind over and over again. This will damage your confidence the next time you're in that position.

Instead, acknowledge the bad break or the mistake you made, and then change subjects in your head by talking about something else, preferably your own or someone else's good performance.

Pre-Competition Visualization

For many bowlers, tournaments are a source of excitement, but also potential anxiety. Effective visualization can decrease your nerves and help you prepare to bowl your best.

When preparing for an important tournament, picture yourself competing with as many relevant details as possible. Include details about the center, such as the settee area and masking units, and the other competitors you expect to see there.

Most importantly, visualize yourself competing and include the lines you might play, the balls you might use, and the success you'll have. Doing this for a few minutes each day leading up to an event will help ease jitters, increase confidence, and improve performance.

A New Perspective on Luck

Think you're an unlucky bowler? Many bowlers do.

Next time you're out on the lanes, try counting all the good breaks you get (lucky strikes, breaking up splits, etc.) alongside all the unlucky breaks.

Even though the bad breaks tend to stand out more in our minds, you'll probably find over time that the number of good breaks and bad breaks is about the same.

This kind of mental exercise will help shift you toward a positive mindset by keeping a better perspective on your "luck."

Using Visualization to Accelerate Skill Acquisition

Visualization is a skill that many bowlers use in their pre-shot routines, or as part of preparing for an important tournament. Did you know that visualization can also be used to help build confidence and speed up skill acquisition? Provided below is a visualization exercise aimed at improving skill development.

While seated comfortably or lying down, picture yourself performing a new or developing skill perfectly:

- Start by picturing the drill in practice, performing several successful repetitions with perfect form.
- Next, picture yourself using that skill perfectly in a full approach, again during practice, free of pressure.
- Finally, imagine yourself bowling in a tournament using that skill. Picture the ball's resulting trajectory, reaction, and impact at the pins for a perfect strike.

Repeat as necessary.

Visualization for Boosting Confidence

While seated comfortably or lying down, picture one of your best bowling performances. Recall the center where you were bowling, the ball(s) you threw, and the people on the pair. Picture your perfect execution for a strike, including the ball motion from the laydown point through the pins. Most importantly, remember the feelings of confidence, control, and freedom of your best performances.

Repeat this process several times per week leading up to an important competition to help build confidence and reinforce your peak performance mindset.

SECTION 5

PRACTICE AND SPARE SHOOTING

Practice makes perfect, or so the saying goes. In truth, practice will only take you as far as it aligns with your goals.

Effective practice can look very different for different people depending on what they want to achieve, but there are some key principles to follow.

Your practice should be:

- **Aligned with your goals**: If you want to improve your swing, you should be focusing on that element of your approach.
- **Aligned with your competition schedule**: You shouldn't be making big changes right before an important tournament.
- **Focused and purposeful**: Eliminate distractions and ensure that you've set a goal for your practice session.

Many bowlers get caught up with the results of their practice. They equate getting strikes to a successful practice session and become frustrated when making a change and the strikes don't come easily.

It's important to stay focused on the process and the item you are working on, whether it is developing your technique, increasing your versatility, or mentally preparing for a tournament. Each of these practices will look different, but they can all be effective.

Of course, in addition to practicing your strikes, spares are still a key part of the game of bowling. Spare shooting alignment and technique can be different from your strike game and should be treated that way.

Practice sessions can and should include spare shooting most of the time, but you can also have a session devoted entirely to spares. In addition, there are many ways to practice spares to provide variety and change the feel.

Whatever your current goals are, make sure that your practice plan is aligned with those goals, that you are putting the work in that's necessary to achieve them, and that you remember to practice your spares.

The Four Phases of Training

When practicing, it's useful to remember the four phases of training and the different areas of focus for each one. You wouldn't make a major overhaul to your approach right before a tournament, would you?

The timing of when to work on things is as important as what you work on:

- **General preparation** is when you will spend your time working on physical elements, breaking things down and doing drills to modify the more permanent elements of your game, such as swing plane, or timing.
- **Specific preparation** is when you will work on skills needed for an upcoming event. This is where the focus shifts to ball reaction and manipulation skills like ball speed, loft, and axis rotation.
- **Pre-competition** is when you start gearing up for a tournament. The focus is more on the mental side of the game and applying your skills. This is where you will start to keep score and make elements of your training more competitive.
- The **competition phase** is when you've stopped working on your game. Practices are short to stay fresh and healthy, while keeping your game sharp.

How Hard Is Your Practice?

Training load is essentially the combination of the volume and the intensity of a given session. In the gym, the volume is the number of reps, while intensity is related to the weights used and the pace of the training.

On the lanes, training load is a bit harder to quantify, but here are some general guidelines:

- Drills, such as an armswing drill or foul line drill, are considered higher volume and lower intensity, because you get a lot more reps in and there's no focus on the actual results at the pins.
- Bowling for score would be considered lower volume but higher intensity, because you are working harder on a mental and tactical level, with fewer shots being taken.
- The closer you get to a competition, the lower the volume and higher the intensity your on-lane practice should be. For example, right before a tournament, you'd be better served by a 30-to-45-minute practice session of competition simulation than by two hours of drills.

The Key Spares to Practice

Every spare is important, but there are some spares that bowlers will leave more often than others. As such, practicing a few key spares will improve your overall spare shooting without overcomplicating your practice routine:

- **Corner pins**: All bowlers should practice their corners, trying to cover both the 4/7 and the 6/10.
- **The 3/6/10 (2/4/7 for lefties)**: This multi-pin combination is extremely commonly left when bowlers go high and miss the pocket.
- **The washout**: Another of the most common multi-pin spares, bowlers should practice hitting the opposite pocket with their spare ball to improve their odds of conversion.

Practicing a cycle of these spares—corner, corner, 3/6/10, washout—will cover a significant portion of your spare shooting needs.

Competition Preparation

Athletes in all sports use training cycles to be at their best in key moments of the year. Bowlers can adopt some of these key concepts to better prepare for important tournaments on their calendars:

- **Training load**: Bowlers should increase their practice four to six weeks before an event, in order to get their game as sharp as possible ahead of the tournament.
- **Tactical and mental training**: Many bowlers focus mostly on physical game issues, but they should spend the last couple of weeks before an event ironing out their mental tools and lane play strategies and skills.
- **Rest up**: The last week before an important tournament should feature the least amount of practice, so your mind and body are in the best shape possible ahead of the competition.

Cross-Training for Bowling

Cross-training is the term used for participating in different sports that allow for better resilience, improved coordination, and complementary skill development. Here are a few things you can do in the off-season away from the lanes that can help set the stage for a successful year:

- Golf is often compared to bowling, and it challenges you in many of the same ways as bowling.
- Walking, jogging, and swimming are great for overall health, and they can improve your endurance on the lanes.
- On rainy days, doing puzzles, solving crosswords, or doing other kinds of mental gymnastics can challenge different areas of focus that you use on the lanes.

As with any physical activity, consult with your health professional before starting any new sport or training activity.

Versatility Training

When it comes to versatility, the ability to use your different skills on demand is extremely important. Based on having a few different skills, here's a fun practice routine to add variety to your training:

- Warm up.
- Bowl a game using each different skill. For example, bowl one game with different hand positions, one game with different speeds, etc.
- Use dice or scrap paper to randomly select a combination of skills, such as "higher speed/lower rotation/medium loft" and try to strike. Then select a different combination and strike again. And so on.

Make sure to only use skills that you've already established, and not the ones that are still a work-in-progress.

Keeping Score During Practice

Whether or not a bowler should keep score in practice depends on the goals of the session. When working on developing your technique or adding a skill, the old advice of ignoring the scoreboard remains true. In fact, it's best to not even have pins if the center has the capacity to do that.

On the other hand, when you are preparing for an event and want to mentally rehearse for the pressures of competition, or ensure that your lane play skills are sharp, keeping score is the only way to gauge your preparation.

Essentially, the more your practice focuses on the physical execution of a skill, the more you should avoid scoring. When your practice focuses on the application of your skills, then keeping score can be an effective method of evaluation.

All-Around Practice Plan

So, you're about a month into the season...you've shaken off some rust, but are you still feeling a bit out of sorts? Aside from a lesson with a certified coach to diagnose a specific problem, you might just need a few reps working on some of the most critical elements of the game.

If you want to practice with a purpose, but you just want to refine your existing game, here's a good general practice plan for all-around improvement in your technique, with a focus on swing and timing mechanics:

- 20 minutes of swing practice, starting with standing swing drills, and then alternating drills and the full approach.
- 20 minutes of timing practice, focusing on the ball start with drills and then alternating with full approaches.
- 20 minutes of spare shooting, including corner pins and a game of Low Ball.

Covering All Your Bases in Practice

Whether it is because you're unsure what to work on next, it's not the right time for a major change, or you just need a bit of a mental break from a grinding practice schedule, practicing with a purpose can be easier said than done.

Here is a good general practice plan that touches on the key elements of your bowling game. It will take approximately one hour to complete. This plan will allow you to work on your overall technique and keep you sharp between tournaments:

- 10 minutes each of ball start drills, swing drills, and release drills, alternating between a drill and then a full approach delivery.
- 10 minutes of spare shooting: corner pins, Low Ball, or any other game or drill designed to improve your spare game.
- One full game for score.

Practicing Your Pre-Shot Routine

Bowlers know they should practice their mental skills, but many are unsure of how to do this in the on-lane practice setting.

The pre-shot routine is made up of several mental tools, such as self-talk and visualization. Regardless of the specific details of your pre-shot routine, here's how you can practice it as part of your on-lane training:

- Start by simply milling around the bowler's area, as if you are waiting your turn. Take your time; you want your mind to wander.
- Perform your pre-shot routine and assume your bowling stance. Stop and put your ball down just as you are ready to take your first step.
- Repeat this process 10 times, allowing as much time as needed between "shots" to allow your brain to reset.

Get even more benefits by having someone time your routines to ensure that each one lasts the same amount of time from start to stance.

Preparing for an Important Event

Athletes in all sports go through training and competition cycles. Many team sports have single peaking seasons, while most individual sports feature several "major" events in a year that top athletes will prioritize. Professional bowlers might target PBA majors, while amateur bowlers might target specific large events in their area.

To peak for these events, bowlers should spend several weeks following this general process:

- **Start slow**: After a break when you've spent less time on the lanes, don't push too hard in your first week back.
- **Build capacity**: Increase your training load to surpass the needs of the tournament. Training for an eight-gamer? Make sure you can bowl up to 10 games at a high level.
- **Taper it off**: In the week before a big event, reduce your training to minimum amounts so that your body and mind are fresh for competition.

Tips for More Effective Practice Sessions

Making the most of practice time is something that all bowlers want to do. Even pros, who have lots more time on the lanes, want that time to be as productive as possible. Whether you practice once a week, once a month, or once a day, good practice habits form the basis of effective skill development.

With this in mind, here are some tips for improving your practice sessions:

- Only bring the equipment you need for that practice. If you are working on skill development, you really only need one ball. More equipment equals more distractions.
- Practice alone. Research indicates that for individual pursuits, the best results come from focused individual practice, not from training in groups. An exception to this would be a lesson with a coach.
- Take breaks when needed and stop practicing when you are no longer productive. This can be after 20 minutes, or it can be after several hours. Quality is more important than quantity.

Challenging Your Versatility

Versatility is an important skill in today's game. In addition to developing the skills to play different areas of the lane and to manipulate ball motion, bowlers need to apply these abilities by challenging their versatility in practice sessions.

Here are a few "games" to play that will challenge you:

- **One Ball, Five Arrows**: The name is self-explanatory, asking you to strike with the same ball across five different arrows. Up the challenge by trying to get five strikes in a row.
- **One Target, All Balls**: The inverse of the first game, use your versatility to strike using every ball you have from the same target line. Time is against you, as the lane breaks down with each shot.
- **New Frame, New Line**: Change balls or lines every frame and bowl your max score.

Practicing With Distractions

Many bowlers try to go to their local bowling center at quiet times and off-hours for focused training sessions. But what if you go to practice and end up beside rowdy open play bowlers or a loud birthday party?

When faced with distractions all around you during a practice session, you should consider modifying your practice plan. Regardless of what you intended to work on, this becomes an opportunity to work on your focus and reframing technique.

First, view this as an opportunity (reframing). Adjust your practice to include focus items, such as doing your pre-shot routine on every shot, starting over if you're interrupted, and performing with loud and unpredictable noises around you. Because it's easy to fall into the trap of trying to "impress" open bowlers and lose all focus, shooting a game of Low Ball for spare practice can help train you to focus on the task at hand, regardless of who is watching.

A Practice Routine for Versatility Training

Coaches regularly tout the value of practicing with a purpose and having a structure to your training. With that in mind, here's a simple practice routine to help develop your versatility skills.

Each segment should last about 10 minutes, or for a single game:

- Warm up.
- Bowl with different hand positions, using one ball.
- Bowl with different balls, using one hand position.
- Spend time shooting spares, preferably corner pins.
- Select the best ball and hand position based on previous observation and bowl a game for score.

Practicing After a Layoff

When starting to get ready for the season after being away from the lanes, try using a practice plan that focuses more on your existing skills and shaking off the rust instead of bowling for score or trying to change something right away.

Try this four-game practice sequence to consolidate your technique after some time away from the lanes:

- **Game 1**: Swing and release drills/full approach deliveries.
- **Game 2**: Focus on tempo and footwork; get things back in sync.
- **Game 3**: Spare shooting; corner pins only.
- **Game 4**: Play a few different lines to practice focusing on alignment.

Spare Shooting 101

Regardless of your skill level, spares are an important part of the game. They can mean the difference between making your average or not, or making the cut at a tournament.

Here are a few tips for improving your spare game:

- **Find a system that works for you**: It's okay to explore a bit, but bowlers need a system to help keep things simple when it comes to spares.
- **Practice, practice, practice**: Devote some time during every practice session to work on some aspect of your spare shooting, whether it is corner pins or multi-pin spares.
- **Change it up**: Challenge yourself by using mini-games or challenges such as Low Ball to keep your training interesting and to help you stay engaged.

Expanding Your Comfort Zone

Not every practice session needs to be focused on physical skills. With the physical foundation already established, it helps to push the boundaries of your comfort zone by practicing in different areas of the lane.

When looking to expand your comfort zone, it's important to make that the focus of your practice, without trying to change anything else. Try the following practice plan once you've warmed up:

- Spend 10 minutes targeting the first arrow, then 10 minutes on the second arrow, and then 10 minutes on the third arrow.
- Spend 10 minutes rotating among all three targets, with one shot on each.
- Bowl one game for score, picking one of the lines that isn't in your typical comfort zone.

More advanced bowlers might use five or even six different arrows to test their skills, but for many bowlers, this three-arrow sequence will be enough to improve your ability to adapt to different conditions.

Alignment for Spare Shooting

Shooting corner pins can be a challenge for many bowlers. More often than not, a bowler struggles with one side while the opposite side poses less of a challenge. Why is that? In many cases, it comes down to body alignment, which is a key point for improving your spare shooting.

Assuming that you already throw the ball straight (or relatively straight) at most of your spares, your physical alignment is very important. Many bowlers are often misaligned for their spare shots, either over-rotating or under-rotating their bodies in the stance, creating problems before they even start the approach.

Square your shoulders, hips, knees, and possibly your feet toward the pin you are trying to hit, not toward your target. Your target (likely an arrow) will probably fall slightly outside the visual path once your body is properly aligned to the corner pin.

The Pre-Spare Routine

The pre-shot routine is a regular theme in mental coaching. For the most part, however, it is discussed only in the context of getting ready for strike shots, and much less time is dedicated to developing a pre-shot routine for spares.

The pre-shot routine includes elements that might need to be adjusted between your strike shots and spare attempts. Your pre-spare routine should include letting go of any negative emotions associated with the first ball, as well as the following elements:

- The choice to park your analysis of the last shot.
- Visualization of the spare target line.
- Self-talk that is specific to spare shooting, such as "hard and straight" or "covered like a blanket."

Spare Shooting Golf

With so many variables in bowling, it can be hard to keep track of the things that really matter to your performance. Spare shooting, however, is one of the easier variables to measure. Keep track of the spares you make and the ones you miss so you know what to work on in your practice sessions.

To make it competitive with yourself or others, try a mini-game of Spare Shooting Golf during your next league night or tournament block. The scoring method is simple: give yourself +2 for missing a single pin, +1 for missing a multi-pin makeable spare, and -1 for converting a split or washout.

At the end of the league night or tournament block, your goal is to have the lowest score possible.

Practice Those Spares

Practice can sometimes be boring, especially when it comes to working on your spares, so you need to change it up in order to stay motivated and engaged.

Here are a few "games" you can play in practice in order to have some fun while improving your spare shooting:

- **Low Ball**: Try to get the lowest score possible by getting no less than one pin on each shot. 20 is a perfect score. Zeroes count as a strike or spare.
- **Spares then Strikes**: Shoot your spare ball first, aiming for a corner pin, and then pick up what's left. 111 is a perfect score.
- **Tough Spare Cycle**: Rather than endlessly shooting corner pins, change it up by adding two other pin combinations that are quite common: the washout and the 3/6/10 (for righthanders). Give yourself five points per converted spare.

Warming Up for League Play

Even though you are most likely bowling on the same oil pattern all year, subtle week-to-week variations in the pattern and the mental benefits of a proper warm-up routine before league should not be underestimated.

Here's an idea of what elements to include in your league night warm-up routine:

- **Dynamic warm-up**: Prior to throwing a ball, bowlers should loosen up their joints and warm up their muscles with dynamic movements.
- **Shoot spares**: If your league custom is to throw one ball per person at a time, make sure to throw a few spare shots at the beginning or end of your warm-up.
- **Start outside**: It's a good habit to throw your first few shots a couple of boards outside of your expected line while you build up your ball speed. The result doesn't matter. Once you're ready, adjust to the lanes as needed.

Mental Practice Tips

Many bowlers know to practice with a purpose and try to focus their on-lane training around a specific element of their physical game. In addition to reading books and learning about the mental game, bowlers should also dedicate time to training their mental skills on the lanes:

- Before even starting your practice, spend five minutes visualizing the drills you intend to perform and the success you wish to have. This develops your visualization skill in addition to creating a positive mindset for practice.
- Devote some time each practice to rehearsing your pre-shot routine. Since the routine is generally under a minute long, you can do several repetitions in a few minutes. This can be a good physical break from a demanding session, and it reinforces your consistency in this skill for competition.
- Becoming distracted during practice is a good opportunity to rehearse your focus. It's often easier to refocus during practice, so take the time to go through a specific refocusing routine that you can use in competition when there is more pressure and more potential for distraction.

Clearing the Rack

This is a game to test your skills made famous by PBA Hall of Famer Mika Koivuniemi. It involves placing all of your bowling balls on the ball return rack and trying to get a strike with each one of them.

The challenge is that you must strike with each ball, but they all have to be used on the same line. So, if you choose to play the third arrow out to board five with Ball A, then you must use that line for every single ball, including your spare ball.

If you get a strike, you get to put that ball back into the bag. The game ends when every ball is off the rack and back in your bag. This is a great test of skill with only one strike, but you can make it harder by trying to get two strikes in a row.

Another wrinkle would be to shoot the spares you leave up whenever you don't strike. If you miss a makeable spare, you must take a ball back out of the bag and put it back on the rack.

Physical Game Practice

Regardless of the technical elements of your game that you are working on, it's best to practice them one at a time.

For example, it will often be more effective to work on your footwork and then to work on your swing direction, than to try to work on both at once. As both improve independently, then you can bring the two together.

With this in mind, here's a sample of how a physical game practice could look.

- Warm up.
- Drills/technique work for Skill A.
- Take a break.
- Drills/technique work for Skill B.
- Practice spare shooting.
- Cool down.

NEXT STEPS

If you've finished all the tips and drills in this book, the question becomes: what's next?

Even professional bowlers are continually working on their games, improving on weaknesses and keeping the best parts of their game sharp.

There are probably a few tips in here that you'll want to re-read on a regular basis. It's easy to forget about the mental cues that help you perform your best, or some of the practice sessions that helped unlock a great performance, for example.

One of the best things you can do for your game is get into a good rhythm with your practices. Whether it's once a week or several times per week, the right training schedule can yield consistently positive performances and improvement.

The goal is to find the plan that works best for you. Some elite bowlers will establish a six-week plan that gets them ready for key tournaments, while others will use four-week or eight-week plans.

Whatever it is that works for you, we hope this book has helped you discover the cues, tips, and drills that will help you continue to improve your game.

ABOUT THE AUTHORS

Tyrel Rose is *Bowling This Month*'s Director of Content. He is the Head Coach for Team Canada, with more than 20 years of experience coaching bowlers of all levels. Tyrel is an NCCP Competition Development level and USBC Bronze Certified coach, and a former Canadian national champion.

Bill Sempsrott is the founder of BTM Digital Media, LLC and he manages the day-to-day operations of *Bowling This Month*. He has a graduate degree in Mechanical Engineering, he developed the *Powerhouse Blueprint* ball motion simulator, and he has been an avid bowler for more than 25 years. He also developed *Bowling Unleashed*, a realistic bowling simulation game for mobile devices.

ABOUT
BOWLING THIS MONTH

Founded in 1994 by Bob Summerville and his wife, Alayne Merenstein, *Bowling This Month* quickly rose to prominence as the only magazine devoted exclusively to the serious bowler. Over the nearly three decades since its inception, *BTM* has become synonymous with a commitment to delivering cutting-edge bowling instructional information to bowlers, coaches, and pro shop operators worldwide.

Bowling This Month publishes in-depth instructional and technical articles covering all aspects of the sport of bowling, including the physical game, mental game, ball motion, drilling and layouts, grip and fitting, health and fitness, lane play, practice techniques, and spare shooting, written by a world-class group of bowling coaches and industry experts with decades of experience studying the sport at its highest levels.

Additionally, *Bowling This Month* was the first bowling publication to print lengthy, independent bowling ball reviews, starting in 1995 and continuing to the present day. *BTM* quickly became known as the go-to source for information on new bowling ball releases and became the trusted bowling ball review partner of countless pro shop operators and bowlers.

Today, *Bowling This Month* lives on as an online magazine, with the same goal as when it was originally founded in 1994: to be the world's best technical resource for serious bowlers. We continue to publish new cutting-edge instructional and technical articles and detailed, unbiased bowling ball reviews. Additionally, our vast online archive of content helps tens of thousands of bowlers around the world learn more about the sport of bowling and improve their games.

If you've enjoyed this book and would like to continue along the path of improving your bowling, we hope you'll consider checking out *Bowling This Month* online and seeing what we have to offer.

Visit us today at www.bowlingthismonth.com.